Coursework

Skills Companion

for
Geography
GCSE

David Payne

www.heinemann.co.uk
✓ Free online support
✓ Useful weblinks
✓ 24 hour online ordering

01865 888058

Inspiring generations

Heinemann Educational Publishers
Halley Court, Jordan Hill, Oxford OX2 8EJ
Part of Harcourt Education

Heinemann is the registered trademark of
Harcourt Education Limited

©Harcourt Education Ltd 2005

First published 2005

09 08 07 06
10 9 8 7 6 5 4 3 2

British Library Cataloguing in Publication Data is available
from the British Library on request.

10-digit ISBN: 0 435340 15 8
13-digit ISBN: 978 0 435340 15 5

Typeset by Thomson Digital
Original illustrations by Tech Type © Harcourt Education Limited, 2004
All photographs appear courtesy of the author.
Cover design by Marcus Bell
Cover photo: © Getty
Printed in the UK by Scotprint
The 'site and situation map set' on pp43 appear courtesy of Cartographic Unit, University
of Southampton.

Every effort has been made to contact copyright holders of material reproduced in this
book. Any omissions will be rectified in subsequent printings if notice is given to the
publishers.

Contents

Icon Key:

Think Icon

Important Point Icon

Safety Icon

Bright Idea Icon

Useful Tip Icon

1 Getting the most out of your coursework

What is coursework?

Coursework is one part of your GCSE Geography assessment and is completed during the course of study. It is worth 25 per cent of your GCSE marks; the remaining 75 per cent of the marks are allocated to the final examinations taken at the end of the course. Your final GCSE grade will be determined by putting together both coursework and examination marks.

What does coursework test?

Coursework tests the following two areas:

⮕ The application of knowledge and understanding.
⮕ The use of geographical skills.

What does this mean?

Testing the 'application of knowledge and understanding' means:

⮕ assessing the level of background knowledge you show about the topic investigated and how well you explained the way your investigation fitted in with the general understanding of the topic
⮕ assessing how well you show that you understood the topic by using the information you collected to explain it
⮕ assessing how well you show that you understood that information is not always reliable or detailed enough to make explanations complete.

Testing the 'use of geographical skills' means:

⮕ assessing how well you identified the information needed to complete your investigation
⮕ assessing how effective you were at collecting information from a number of different sources
⮕ assessing how well you presented information through the use of a variety of techniques
⮕ assessing how well you identified the main points from your collected information.

Use your coursework to show the examiner what you know and can do!

Can I study anything for my coursework?

The most important point to consider is that your Geography coursework must look at a topic that is part of your Geography course. In most cases, your teacher will have checked this for you, but if you want to see where your coursework topic fits in with the overall course, look at the examination specification. To find out more about the AQA examination specification, go to www. Heinemann.co.uk/hotlinks, insert the express code 0158P.

Other points to think about

⮕ Geography coursework must be geographical! It must relate to a place.
⮕ Although coursework investigations often look at change, be careful that your investigation is not totally set in the past and is really a history project!

What are the advantages of coursework?

Although completing coursework can be quite time consuming and hard work, it has many advantages, some of which are shown below.

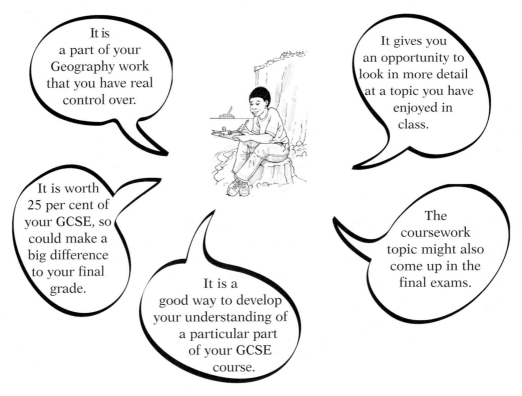

It is a part of your Geography work that you have real control over.

It gives you an opportunity to look in more detail at a topic you have enjoyed in class.

It is worth 25 per cent of your GCSE, so could make a big difference to your final grade.

It is a good way to develop your understanding of a particular part of your GCSE course.

The coursework topic might also come up in the final exams.

Completing coursework involves collecting information outside of school, so always:
- ➲ listen to advice about safety
- ➲ discuss any individual data collection plans with teachers and parents
- ➲ don't go to places alone
- ➲ keep people informed about what you are doing.

How will your coursework be marked?

Your coursework will be marked by using a mark scheme which identifies **five** areas for assessment (called assessment criteria). The table below lists the five assessment criteria and explains briefly what each of them means. You can score up to six marks in each of the five criteria giving a maximum total of thirty marks. Each section has the same number of marks and so all sections are equally important. As you work through your investigation, check it against the mark scheme and identify its strengths and weaknesses.

Assessment criteria

Applied understanding	Have you described what part of your GCSE course is being investigated? How does your investigation develop an understanding of your chosen topic? Is the location of your investigation clearly identified?
Methodology	Is the information collected clearly linked to the original idea? Have you explained why you needed the information you collected? Have you described where and how you collected your information?
Data presentation	Have you used a number of different presentation methods? Are some of your presentation methods quite complex? Has information and communications technology (ICT) been used to present some or all of your investigation? Have you used precise and accurate language?
Data interpretation	Have you identified the main points from your data collection? Have you clearly explained what your information shows in relation to the topic? Have you explained and developed any links between the information collected? Are your conclusions clearly linked to your original idea?
Evaluation	Were there any limitations or problems with your data collection? How accurate were your results? How realistic are your conclusions? Have you considered how accuracy and limitations of data collection may have affected your conclusions?

How is the mark decided in each area?

Each of the five assessment criteria is divided into three levels, with each level having two marks, for example:

Level 1 is worth 1 or 2 marks   Lowest level

Level 2 is worth 3 or 4 marks   ↓

Level 3 is worth 5 or 6 marks   Highest level

What does the coursework mark scheme look like?

The examination board produces a mark scheme which describes what is expected in order to achieve the mark in each level. The table shows a simplified version of the mark scheme – please refer to the AQA examination specification for a full copy.

The mark scheme

	Level 1 (1–2 marks)	Level 2 (3–4 marks)	Level 3 (5–6 marks)
Applied understanding	Brief description of location General understanding of the topic Some geographical language	Investigation effectively located General background understanding clearly applied to the topic Use of geographical language	Detailed locational understanding Thorough description and understanding of the ideas applied to the topic Uses a wide range of geographical language
Methodology	Basic links between the topic and data collection Lists methods of data collection Limited range of basic techniques	Data collection clearly linked to the topic Describes data collection methods Good range of appropriate techniques	Data collection has detailed links to the topic Describes and explains the relevance of data collection methods Wide range of appropriate techniques Evidence of originality and initiative
Data presentation	Limited range of methods Reasonable level of accuracy	Use of number of methods Accurate use of language Use of ICT skills	Uses a wide range of methods, including some complex skills Precise and accurate use of language Uses ICT to present information
Data interpretation	Brief description of results	Good description of results Gives meaning to the results Some concluding points	Detailed description of results with clear reasons Draws out links between data Concluding points linked to original title
Evaluation	Some appreciation of how the investigation could be improved Comments on the reliability of the methods	Clear appreciation of how the investigation could be improved Comments on the reliability of the methods Comments on the accuracy of the results	Comments on the reliability of the methods Comments on the accuracy of the results Comments on the validity of the conclusion

2 Getting started: the road to success

What are coursework investigations?

Coursework investigations are usually one of the following:

➲ Teacher-led investigations.
➲ Teacher-guided investigations with some individual development.
➲ Individual investigations.

Teacher-led investigations

In teacher-led investigations students are given the topic and the data collection is usually organised by the teacher. Students very often have similar data which means that the investigations can look similar and lack originality and initiative.

If you are completing a teacher-led investigation, ask your teacher for ideas about how you might extend your topic to include some original or different data. This will give your investigation some originality which will give you the opportunity to score higher marks in the methodology section. It might also give you better opportunities for data presentation and analysis!

Teacher-guided investigations with some individual development

In these types of investigation students are often given the topic, and some of the data collection is organised by the teacher. Students can then add to the data by collecting additional information.

If you are completing this type of investigation, make sure that any additional information is linked to the original topic. Also, additional information should not simply repeat the original data collection methods; always give reasons for using different methods. You could re-visit the site and collect different data or apply the techniques to a comparable site.

Individual investigations

Individual investigations are chosen by the student (usually after discussion with a teacher) and carried out by the student collecting totally individual information. Individual investigations can often be very imaginative and score high marks.

If you are carrying out an individual investigation you will need to make sure that:
- ⊃ the topic is closely linked to the course
- ⊃ you have easy and safe access to the study area
- ⊃ the topic fits the mark scheme and allows you to score marks in each of the assessment criteria
- ⊃ the investigation is not too large and can be completed in a reasonable amount of time
- ⊃ the wording of any investigation is not too broad and therefore impossible to prove.

Always seek your teacher's advice, especially when you are completing an individual investigation.

Using ICT

The use of ICT in your investigation is compulsory and you will need to use at least two different ICT techniques.

Information and communications technology (ICT) can be a very useful tool when collecting information and will help you present your work effectively.

Some of the ways you can use ICT to help you include:
- ⊃ using the Internet to obtain background information which will increase your understanding of the topic being investigated
- ⊃ using the Internet to find secondary sources or contacts.
- ⊃ organising your collected information
- ⊃ scanning in data or digital photographs
- ⊃ data presentation (maps, graphs etc).
- ⊃ word processing and presenting your final investigation.

Useful website links

Websites can be used to find: local planning information, traffic data, environmental information, tourism data, general location maps, detailed maps and plans, population data, and so on.

When researching websites, stick to the topic and don't waste time browsing!

A general plan of action

Always have the **mark scheme** in your mind – you don't want to spend time producing what looks like an excellent investigation only to be told that it does not fit the mark scheme.

Getting started

- Think about what you have been studying in Geography lessons.
- Look at the outline of the whole of the Geography GCSE course.
- What areas of the Geography course are you particularly interested in?
- Are there any local developments or issues that might make an interesting investigation?

Build up a glossary of geographical terms as you research your coursework topic.

Background to the topic

- Although your investigation may be based in your local area, you will find it helpful to do some general background reading on the topic.
- Make a note of any important geographical words or definitions linked to the topic and any useful sources of information.

Think about the information you need

- The information you collect must be appropriate to your investigation. Ask yourself the question, 'What information do I need to reach a conclusion?'
- Do a brainstorm or have a discussion with friends about your topic – this will help to identify the information you need.

Obtaining the information you need

Collecting lots of irrelevant information will not score you many marks!

- There are many ways to obtain information, but remember that data collection has to be manageable.
- You can collect new information by counting, measuring, asking or observing.
- Existing information can be collected from books, newspapers, websites, and so on.

Presenting and analysing your information

This is where the quality of your data collection begins to show!

If you have collected a wide range of data:

- you will have the opportunity to use a range of presentation techniques
- you will have plenty to say about the topic being investigated.

Coming to a conclusion

⊃ Return to your original idea – it is often helpful to re-state the original idea.

⊃ Identify the most important points from your data collection and link these to your original idea.

⊃ Use the information you have collected to reach a conclusion.

⊃ Make some observations about how well your investigation worked.

⊃ Describe any limitations of your investigation.

⊃ Consider how your investigation might be improved.

How to choose a topic

There are a number of questions to consider when choosing a topic for your coursework investigation, including the following.

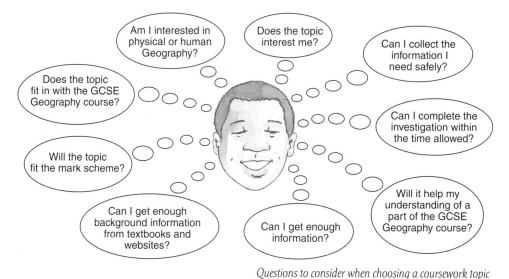

Questions to consider when choosing a coursework topic

- Always be aware of the dangers of collecting information in physical environments.
- Always discuss any individual data collection with your teachers and parents.
- It is always better to collect information with someone else.
- Keep people informed of where you are going to collect information.

A good range of information will get you good marks for data collection and give you excellent opportunities for using a number of presentation techniques. It will also give you plenty to say about your results!

Writing a successful investigation

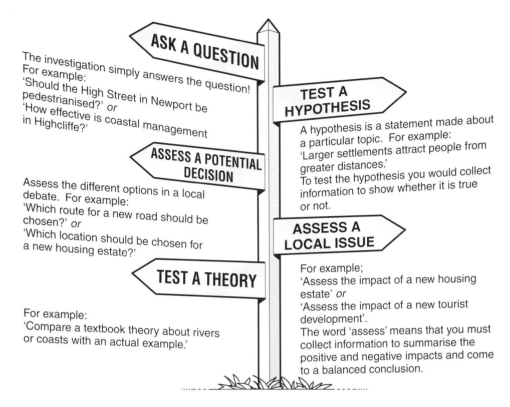

ASK A QUESTION

The investigation simply answers the question!
For example:
'Should the High Street in Newport be pedestrianised?' or
'How effective is coastal management in Highcliffe?'

ASSESS A POTENTIAL DECISION

Assess the different options in a local debate. For example:
'Which route for a new road should be chosen?' or
'Which location should be chosen for a new housing estate?'

TEST A THEORY

For example:
'Compare a textbook theory about rivers or coasts with an actual example.'

TEST A HYPOTHESIS

A hypothesis is a statement made about a particular topic. For example:
'Larger settlements attract people from greater distances.'
To test the hypothesis you would collect information to show whether it is true or not.

ASSESS A LOCAL ISSUE

For example;
'Assess the impact of a new housing estate' or
'Assess the impact of a new tourist development'.
The word 'assess' means that you must collect information to summarise the positive and negative impacts and come to a balanced conclusion.

The definition of a successful investigation

Test your idea by discussing it with friends or family. They may know people who could help you.

- If a hypothesis is too broad or general, it will be impossible to prove or disprove it!
- Choose a topic of appropriate scale. If the scale is too big, for example the impact of tourism in Cornwall, your investigation may end up looking too general. If the scale is too small, you might struggle to find enough information.

Making a start on your chosen topic

If you are testing a hypothesis, it should be part of the title.

Having chosen, or been given a topic for your investigation, you will then need to make a start. It is often useful to spend some time thinking about a number of key questions which are important to all investigations, and then putting together a plan of action. This should include a list of things to be done and some idea of when each should be completed.

Key questions

1 **What is the title of your investigation?** The title is the first thing the examiner sees, so it needs to say exactly what the investigation is about. It is often helpful to include some locational or place context in the title.

2 **Where is the area of study?** Is your investigation about a particular place, a part of a town or a general area? Identify the specific area you are investigating by looking at Ordnance Survey maps or town plans.

3 **What are the key ideas and words associated with your investigation?** Use a blank sheet of paper and 'brainstorm' your topic by writing down all the ideas and words you can think of. For example, if you are carrying out a shopping investigation, the following points might be useful:

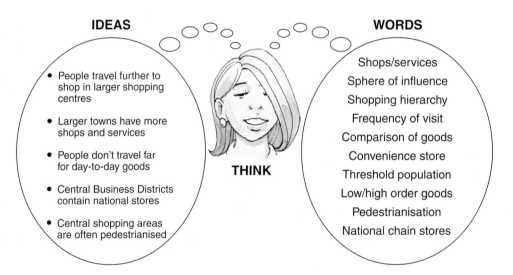

IDEAS

- People travel further to shop in larger shopping centres
- Larger towns have more shops and services
- People don't travel far for day-to-day goods
- Central Business Districts contain national stores
- Central shopping areas are often pedestrianised

THINK

WORDS

Shops/services
Sphere of influence
Shopping hierarchy
Frequency of visit
Comparison of goods
Convenience store
Threshold population
Low/high order goods
Pedestrianisation
National chain stores

4 **Where can you find background information for your topic?** Use textbooks, local newspapers, websites and any local information to identify important points. Add any new ideas or words to your original 'brainstorm' sheet.

Plan of action

Use a time plan like the one below and try to stick to it. Be realistic, you do have other commitments!

> Choose a topic that is part of your GCSE Geography course. It is important to show that you have detailed knowledge of the subject.

⇩

> Do some background reading to identify the main ideas and geographical words associated with your investigation.

⇩

> Geography is about place, so make sure you identify the location of your study – a general location map is always helpful.

⇩

> Identify the information required to carry out your investigation.

⇩

> Collect primary and secondary data, making notes about how you did it.

⇩

> Present your collected information and explain what it shows.

⇩

> Come to a conclusion and write an evaluation.

Title of investigation:	
Action	**Complete by:**
Background reading	
Primary data	
Secondary data	
Introduction	
Methodology	
Data presentation and interpretation	
Conclusion and evaluation	
Finishing touches	

Don't leave your work until the last minute!

Let your teacher see your work as it progresses.

3 Collecting and presenting information

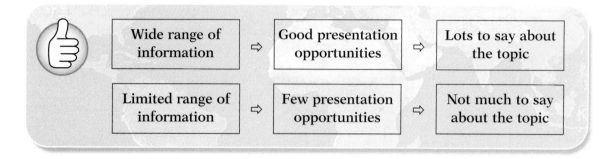

Primary and secondary data

There are two main types of information – usually called data – and these are shown in the table below.

The differences between primary and secondary data

Type of data	Definition	Examples
Primary Data	Original information collected first-hand by fieldwork	Measuring Counting Assessing Interviewing Sketch mapping Taking photographs
Secondary Data	Information from published sources which was collected by someone else	Census data Textbooks Planning documents Local Newspapers Leaflets Maps Directories Websites Photographs

The most successful studies use secondary data to show a general understanding of the topic and primary data to link it to a local area.

Where should you start?

In order to get the highest marks for your data collection, the data *must* be linked to your study and not simply collected for the sake of it.

Asking yourself the following two questions is a good place to start:

1 What information do I need to address my title?
2 Why is my information important to my investigation?

Start with a brainstorming exercise like the one below. This will tell you if the title is useful and give you an idea about the possible range of opportunities for data collection.

When collecting data always make a note of when and where you collected it – and if there were any problems!

Title of investigation: Should St James's Street be pedestrianised?

What information might be useful?	Why might the information be useful?
Traffic flow data	To see how busy St James's Street is. If St James's Street is pedestrianised, the traffic will have to use other roads
Land-use survey	To see if the area is part of the Central Business District, an area which is pedestrianised in many town centres
Pedestrian count	To see how many people use the area.
Questionnaire	To get people's views about traffic problems and pedestrianisation in the area.

Using Ordnance Survey (OS) maps

Ordnance Survey (OS) maps are available at different scales and can be used to locate the general area of your investigation and to prepare a detailed base map. The most useful types of OS map available are shown in the table below.

Type of map	Scale	General description
Superplan	1:2500	Very detailed street map with individual houses, shops and industries shown
Landplan	1:10000	Shows general land use and identifies rural/urban differences
Explorer	1:25000	Shows general urban/rural patterns and detailed physical features
Landranger	1:50000	Covers a large area and shows general patterns. Useful to show the location of your investigation

To find out more about **OS maps**, go to www.heinemann.co.uk/hotlinks, insert the express code 0158P, and click on this topic.

Questionnaires

Questionnaires are an excellent source of primary data and can be used to obtain information about:

- ➲ People's habits
- ➲ People's views
- ➲ People's opinions.

You will find it helpful to have a letter from school on headed notepaper explaining what you are doing when questioning people.

Constructing a questionnaire

A questionnaire must be carefully planned if it is going to give useful data. It is not just about asking questions, **but about asking appropriate questions!**

In order to produce an effective questionnaire, you need to consider the following points:

- ➲ What types of information do you need in order to complete your investigation?
- ➲ How does each question relate to your investigation?
- ➲ Are you going to ask the questions directly or ask people to fill in the questionnaires?

What types of information can you obtain?

- ➲ Background data about the respondents. For example:
  - – age and sex of respondents (people who answer questionnaires)
  - – occupational data.
- ➲ Activity data about what people do. For example:
  - – how often people go shopping
  - – how often people visit a park
  - – what facilities people use the most.
- ➲ Attitudinal data – what people think about a particular issue. For example:
  - – Do you think a new road should be built?
  - – What do you think about the environmental quality of an area?
  - – Do you think a particular place needs more facilities?
  - – Do you think a particular coastal area is well managed?

If respondents are given a questionnaire to fill in by themselves, the questions need to be very clear.

Questions can give objective (facts) information and subjective (opinions) information. For example, 'How often do you use this facility' will give you factual information, whereas 'What do you think about the quality of the shops in this area?' will give you the respondent's opinion.

Avoid asking personal questions which might offend people, such as 'How old are you?' or 'How much do you earn?'

The most successful questionnaires are often a mixture of closed and open questions.

How can you get personal data?

- When asking questions make a note of the sex and approximate age of the respondents (young/middle aged/older).
- Make personal questions less intrusive by offering a broad choice of options. For example:
'How old are you? Tick one box.
☐ 15 – 25 ☐ 26 – 40 ☐ 41 – 55 ☐ 56 – 65 ☐ Over 65

Types of questions

The types of question you ask will be determined by whether you need lots of simple data or a limited amount of more detailed data. The two main types of question are:

- closed questions
- open questions.

Closed questions

These are short-answer questions, often with a yes/no or tick box response. They are an excellent way of collecting lots of information very quickly but do not give detailed responses.

Open questions

These are longer questions where respondents can make longer, general comments. They can provide considerable detail but can take a long time, and answers may be subjective (opinions) rather than factual.

How long should a questionnaire be?

The length of a questionnaire will depend upon what you are trying to find out, but usually a questionnaire should not have more than ten questions. Questionnaires with mainly open questions tend to have fewer questions.

How should you lay out a questionnaire?

The most successful questionnaires usually start with several closed questions which gather general information and end with a limited number of open questions.

When doing questionnaires or interviews make sure your teacher and parents know what you are doing, and always work in pairs.

Use a round number of questionnaires (for example 10, 20, 50). This will make it easier for you to work out percentages and pie charts.

"And now for question 94"

Should you try out the questionnaire?

It is always a good idea to make sure your questionnaire works by testing or piloting it on a small number of people (especially if you intend giving out a written questionnaire). If it works well, then you can use it on a larger number of people, or adjust any questions that do not seem to work.

How many people should you ask?

You are going to draw conclusions from the people you ask, so you need to get enough evidence to be sure that your results are a true representation of the general population. Consequently, you will need what is called a 'representative sample'. For a shopping survey this might mean between 50 and 100 people; for a small village study, 10 to 20 people might be a reasonable representative sample. The number of people you ask might also be determined by the type of questions. If your questionnaire has only closed questions, you could ask a large number of people in a short time.

How do you select the people to ask?

Selecting people to answer a questionnaire is called sampling. You cannot ask everybody, so you need to select or sample a number of people.

- ⮑ The type of people you ask must reflect your investigation. For example, in a study about car parking problems asking non-drivers or very young people might be of limited use.
- ⮑ If your investigation affects the whole community but you only ask young people questions you will not get a very representative sample.

When you write up your investigation explain how you decided the number and type of people to ask.

There are three main types of sampling:

- ⮑ **Random sampling** – where each member of a population has an equal chance of being selected. For example, in a street questionnaire every house number is put in a bag and ten are selected at random.
- ⮑ **Stratified sampling** – where the proportion of respondents is selected according to the topic. For example, in a questionnaire about youth club facilities it might make more sense to ask a larger proportion of younger people.
- ⮑ **Systematic sampling** – where a regular sample is taken. For example, every tenth person, every fifth house, every ten metres.

Examples of questionnaires

Questionnaires A and B were used for shopping investigations. Look carefully at them and identify their strengths and weaknesses.

Questionnaire A

1 How old are you?
2 How often do you come here?
3 Where do you live?
4 How did you get here?
5 How far did you travel to get here?
6 Do you think the bus service is good?
7 What are you buying today?
8 Do you think the town is good for shopping?

EXAMINER'S COMMENT

1 Very personal
2 What does 'often' mean here?
3 Address? Town?
4 Could give options
5 Can work this out from question 3
6 Is this relevant?
7 Vague and personal
8 Vague and general

Questionnaire B

Observe Sex: (M/F)   Age: (Young/Middle-aged/Older)

1 How often do you visit this area?
 ☐ Daily
 ☐ 2-3 times a week
 ☐ Once a week
 ☐ Less often

2 Which town/village did you come from today?

3 How did you travel here today?
 ☐ Walk
 ☐ Bus
 ☐ Car
 ☐ Other

4 Are you using any of the following services today?
 ☐ Bank/building society
 ☐ Bookshop
 ☐ Clothing shop
 ☐ Electrical goods shop
 ☐ Furniture shop
 ☐ Post office
 ☐ Travel agent

5 How do you rate the following? (1 = very poor; = 5 excellent)
 The variety of shops   ☐
 The quality of goods in shops   ☐
 Leisure facilities (cafes, etc.)   ☐
 The general environment   ☐

Try to use a range of different methods to present your questionnaire results.

Presenting questionnaire data

The methods you choose to present your questionnaire data will be determined by the types of questions you have asked. The following techniques are frequently used to present information obtained from questionnaires:

- ➲ bar charts
- ➲ pie charts
- ➲ pictograms
- ➲ desire line map.

Bar charts

The length of each bar represents the quantity of each component. For example:

Question: How did you travel here today?

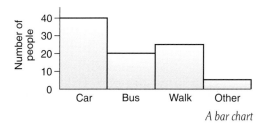

A bar chart

Pie chart

A pie chart shows the percentage of each component. It is easier to calculate this if a round number of questionnaires was used (for example 50,100). For example:

Question: How often do you visit this area?

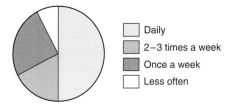

A pie chart

Pictograms

Pictograms are picture graphs where the picture gives a visual representation of the data. For example:

Question: How did you travel here today?

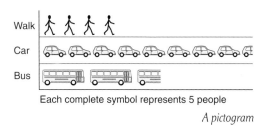

Each complete symbol represents 5 people

A pictogram

Desire line map

A desire line map is drawn to show the movement of people, either individually or in groups. For example:

Question: Which town/village did you come from today?

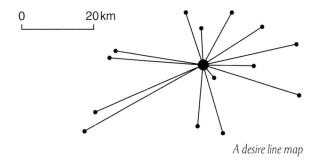

A desire line map

Places could be added if location is important.

Questionnaire information can also be presented as a table of figures.

Conducting interviews

Interviews are like questionnaires but usually have open questions where people can say quite a lot. Investigations should only have a limited number of interviews with people who are very important to the overall investigation.

The key to a successful interview is preparation. Think carefully about what you need to find out and prepare precise questions in advance.

Interviews can give you objective data (facts) and subjective data (opinions). Be careful to separate **facts** from **opinions** when you analyse the comments.

It is often helpful to tape an interview but *always* ask permission first!

Presenting information from interviews

You will often gain a great deal of information from an interview; some of which may not be that important. Identify the points that are important to your investigation by using a highlighter pen. The important points can then be presented in the form of a table or as speech bubbles.

The example below shows the results of an interview carried out with a shop manager concerning the possible pedestrianisation of a main shopping area.

'There is no doubt that it will improve the general environment'

'It could bring more people into the area to shop and consequently create more business'

'It will certainly cause enormous disruption while it is being carried out'

'Increased business might mean I need more staff'

'The area will need more litter bins and cleaners because pedestrianised areas often generate more litter'

'It could cause a problem for deliveries since we don't have a rear entrance for deliveries'

Interview with a shop manager

Shopping quality surveys

Many investigations compare town centres or assess the quality of different parts of a town centre. This information can be used to find out why people are attracted to certain areas or as part of an investigation about identifying the Central Business District (CBD) in a town.

A shopping quality survey can take into account a number of factors including types and quality of shops and the general land use in an area. In the example below four factors are rated on a scale from 1 to 3, then added together to give a total quality value. The final score can range from 4 (lowest quality) to 12 (highest quality).

Shopping quality survey

Give each factor a rating from 1 (lowest quality) to 3 (highest quality)

General land use ☐

1   Mixture of shops, services and offices
2   Shops and financial services
3   Mainly shops

Type of shop ☐

1   Smaller shops, mainly local
2   Mainly smaller shops, some local
3   Large department stores, national stores

Range of goods ☐

1   Small range of low-cost goods
2   Average range of goods
3   Wide range of goods

Quality of goods ☐

1   Low quality/low-price goods
2   Mixed quality/range of prices
3   Good quality/designer goods

Presenting shopping quality information

Shopping quality information can be presented by proportional symbol maps and enhanced with the use of photographs.

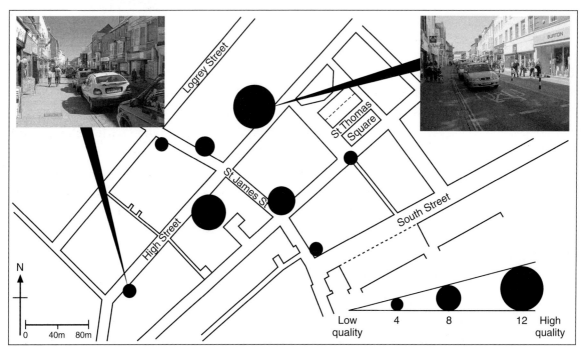

A proportional symbol map

Land-use surveys

You can often get useful base maps from the local authority planning office, Ordnance Survey or local estate agents.

There are three main types of land-use survey:

- generic land-use survey
- detailed land-use survey
- land-use transect.

Generic land-use survey

This type of survey identifies the general land use in an area such as:

- commercial
- residential
- industrial
- agriculture.

It is useful in general planning and issue-based investigations such as 'Should a new housing estate be built in a particular area?'

A land-use transect will often be helpful in investigations identifying CBDs or comparing real places with land-use models. It can also be used to show residential changes in an area.

When carrying out a land-use survey, identify whether the shops/services are national chain stores or local businesses. This is often useful if you are trying to identify the CBD in a town.

Detailed land-use survey

This type of survey identifies the use of particular buildings or types of shops/services in a town centre. This type of land-use survey is helpful when completing investigations about shopping habits, identifying Central Business Districts (CBDs) or topics linked to the management of town centres.

Land-use transect

A land-use transect is a survey along a particular line or road. It is a useful way to see how buildings and land use change with distance, and it can be used in both urban and rural investigations.

In urban areas a number of transects can be studied from the centre of a town to show how land use changes as you move from the centre towards the outskirts. It is often more manageable if you identify roads that radiate out from a town centre as a starting point.

Presenting land-use information

Land-use map

When completing a town centre land-use map you cannot show every different shop or service. You will need to identify the main categories like the example below:

A land-use map

To find out more about town centre building-use maps, go to www.heinemann.co.uk/hotlinks, insert the express code 0158P, and click on this topic.

Land-use transect

Land-use along a transect can be recorded on a map or by using a
sketch or photographs. If you use a sketch or photographs, make sure
the position of your transect is located on a map.

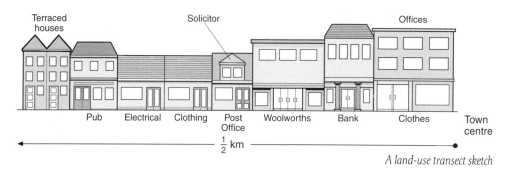

A land-use transect sketch

When completing a transect always make sure you have some idea
of the relative size of buildings and the overall length of the
transect. Building height is also important because buildings are
generally taller closer to town centres.

Pedestrian counts

**Make sure all
of your
pedestrian
counts are
conducted
over the same
time period.**

Pedestrian counts are a useful source of data and can be used in a
number of ways including:

➲ comparing pedestrian flows in different parts of a town centre
➲ comparing pedestrian flows in different town centres
➲ comparing pedestrian flows at different times
➲ assessing the link between pedestrian flows and land use
➲ assessing the link between pedestrian flows and distance from a town
centre
➲ assessing the use of recreational facilities in areas of tourism.

➲ The number of pedestrian counts taken and the time of day
will influence your results. The more data you collect, the more
reliable the results will be.
➲ Always explain why you selected the locations to conduct your
pedestrian counts.

Presenting pedestrian flow data

Two different ways of presenting pedestrian flow data are shown below:

➲ proportional bar map
➲ isoline map.

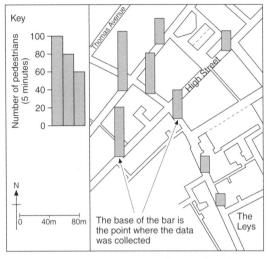

A proportional bar map

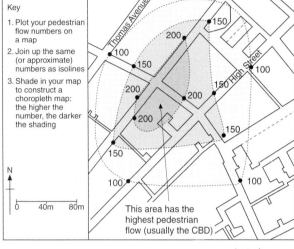

An isoline map

Traffic flow surveys

Always select a safe place to collect data.

Traffic flow surveys record the total flow of traffic or the different types of traffic using particular roads.

Traffic flow data can be used to identify a number of factors, including:

➲ differences in traffic flow
➲ roads where there are congestion problems
➲ roads where there are potential hazards
➲ tourist areas (honey pots) where there are seasonal traffic pressures.

Constructing a data collection sheet, like the one below, will make data collection easier and more accurate.

Cars	Motor-cycles	Cycles	Lorries	Buses/ coaches
LH1 LH1	111	1	1111	11

Date . . . .   Time . . . .
Location . . . .   Weather . . . .

To find out more about **traffic flow data**, go to www.heinemann.co.uk/hotlinks, insert the express code 0158P, and click on this topic.

Presenting traffic flow data

Flow line maps are a good way of showing traffic flows along roads. The width of the line is drawn in proportion to the number of vehicles and an arrow gives the direction of flow.

The time of day will influence your results, so try to do your traffic counts at different times to give a more accurate picture.

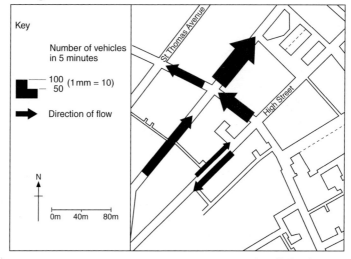

A traffic flow line map

Car parking surveys are often useful sources of data collection, especially in shopping or town centre investigations.

Assessing residential quality

Estate agents often have maps of residential areas and details about houses in different areas, such as price, type of house, quality, and so on.

Assessing the residential quality of different areas in a town can be time consuming, and using a questionnaire is often difficult because it is a very personal matter. In order to collect information an observation quality index (like the one on page 27) can be used, together with photographs. Total scores will range from 5 (very poor) to 25 (very good).

An observation quality index

	1 Very poor	2 Poor	3 Average	4 Good	5 Very Good
Quality of decoration (paintwork, etc.)					
General maintenance (windows/roofs, etc.)					
Garden (tidy)					
Quality of open spaces (green areas/play areas)					
Traffic safety (cars on pavements, etc.)					

Be aware that observation data can be very subjective!

The use of annotated photographs is helpful when comparing residential areas.

Presenting residential quality information

Residential quality information can be presented either in a table of figures or on a proportional symbol map. The information must always be located to show exactly where it was collected.

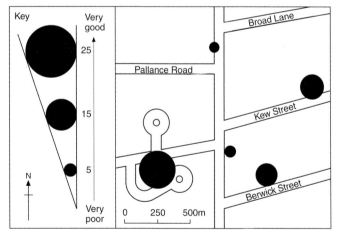

A proportional symbol map showing residential quality information

Assessing environmental quality

Many investigations require an assessment of environmental quality. The word 'environment' can include a number of factors including:

- ⮑ street quality in towns or villages
- ⮑ countryside quality in rural or recreational areas
- ⮑ residential areas
- ⮑ public parks or children's play areas
- ⮑ footpaths.

Always locate the positions of your data collection on a base map.

One of the most successful ways of assessing environmental quality is by using a technique called 'bi-polar analysis'. (Bi-polar means 'two poles' or opposites.)

To construct a bi-polar grid you will need to identify the key points you want to assess and work out the positive and negative aspects of each of them. For example, in order to assess different areas of a town centre the bi-polar grid below might be useful.

Bi-polar grid

Negative pole	−2	−1	0	+1	+2	Positive pole
Lots of traffic pollution		✓				No traffic pollution
Lots of litter	✓					No litter
Ugly buildings	✓					Attractive buildings
Lots of vandalism		✓				No vandalism
No landscaping	✓					Good landscaping
TOTAL SCORE = −8						

Having identified the factors you wish to assess, simply tick the appropriate boxes. In this example the area assessed scored a total of –8, which means the environmental quality is poor.

- ⮑ Carry out a number of environmental quality surveys in order to identify differences.
- ⮑ You can analyse your data by comparing totals or looking at individual parts of the survey.

Presenting environmental quality information

Environmental quality information can be presented using similar techniques to residential quality information, such as proportional symbol maps.

The use of annotated photographs is helpful when describing environmental quality. Use the photographs to identify the positive and negative characteristics of the environment.

Assessing noise pollution

You do not always need to use complex equipment to assess noise pollution, a simple number/description grid like the one below will often give a good impression of noise levels. Do a number of noise surveys in different areas to be able to make comparisons.

Noise pollution grid

Noise level	Description
1	Can hear a whisper
2	Can hear normal conversation
3	Can hear raised voices
4	Have to shout to be heard
5	Cannot hear conversation

To find out more about **environmental data**, go to www.heinemann.co.uk/hotlinks, insert the express code 0158P, and click on this topic.

Visual interpretation – field sketches and photographs

Field sketches and photographs are an excellent way of showing information and are particularly useful in physical geography investigations where it might be difficult to find sufficient primary data.

Always locate the position of your field sketches or photographs on a base map. You can use an arrow to show the direction you were looking when you drew your sketch or took the photograph.

Field sketching

Field sketching is a difficult skill, but remember that you are not trying to produce a work of art!

A field sketch gives you the opportunity to:

➲ observe and record what is around you

➲ include what is relevant to your investigation and leave out what is not.

How to draw field sketches

1 Decide the precise area you are going to draw and stick to it!
2 Divide your paper into the key parts. For a physical sketch, that might be the horizon, middle distance and foreground. For an urban sketch, it might be the dominant buildings.
3 Put the main lines/details in first.
4 Don't worry too much about fine detail.
5 When complete add shading and annotated notes to identify the key points.

You can draw a sketch from a photograph – including only the points you need!

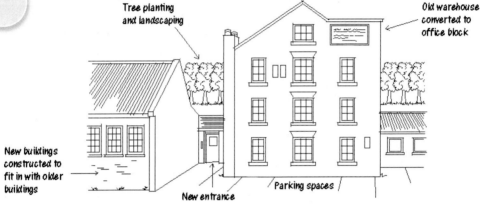

A field sketch

Photographs

Digital photography can be an excellent way of both collecting and presenting information, but you will need to consider the following:

⮑ Why is the photograph useful to my investigation?
⮑ How can the photograph be used to make particular points?
⮑ How am I going to show where the photograph was taken and the direction the camera was pointing?

Using photographs successfully

Annotated photographs are a good way to show ICT skills.

1 Don't use too many photographs – your investigation should not look like a photo album!

2 Select the photographs to be used carefully – each one must make a descriptive or analytical point.

3 You must 'use' each photograph by linking it to your investigation and using annotations to identify the key points.

The example on page 31 was taken from an investigation about coastal processes and how they are managed.

Beach used for recreation

Concrete sea wall

Groynes built to reduce longshore drift

Shingle beach

Wave cut platform

Chalk headland

Stack

Caves

Freshwater Bay – using a photograph in an investigation

Investigating physical geography

While the majority of students complete an investigation which is focused on the relationship between people and their environment, it is acceptable to produce a purely physical investigation as long as it relates specifically to a part of your GCSE Geography course.

Physical investigations often focus on river or coastal processes and frequently compare actual landscapes with textbook theory.

The following examples illustrate the potential for river or coastal investigations.

River investigations

Examples of river investigations

Hypothesis	Method
The width, depth and cross-sectional area of a river will increase with distance from its source	(a) Measure the width and average depth of a river (b) Calculate cross-sectional area by multiplying width by average depth Width Calculate average depth
River velocity increases with distance from its source	Velocity can be measured by a flow meter or by timing a float over a short length of a river
River bedload becomes smaller and more rounded with distance from its source	Take a sample of pebbles at a number of sites and assess their size, shape and roundness
The shape of a river valley changes downstream	Measure the width and depth of a river and the angle of the valley sides using a clinometer or protractor Angle Width Depth

Data collection

⮑ Select a number of sample sites (A-E) along a small stream or river. An Ordnance Survey map (1:25000) might be helpful.

⮑ At each site collect the appropriate data.

⮑ Take photographs or complete sketches to illustrate the data collection methods and the physical characteristics at each site.

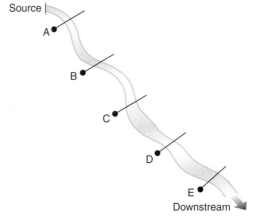

Points for data collection marked on a stream

To find out more about rivers go to www.heinemann.co.uk/hotlinks, insert the express code 0158P, and click on this topic.

Coastal investigations

Examples of coastal investigations

Hypothesis	Method
Material is moved along a beach by wave action	(a) Throw a float into the sea and plot its course over a period of time. (b) Place painted pebbles on a beach and map their location. Try and find them after the next high tide to assess their movement. (c) If the beach has groynes, measure the cross profile of the beach to illustrate beach movement.
Beach material varies from the front to the back of a beach	(a) Select a number of transects from the shoreline to the back of the beach (b) Measure the gradient of each transect using a clinometer or protractor (c) Sample and record the size and shape of beach material along each transect
The shape of a cliff is determined by rock type	(a) Identify the cliff material from a geological map (b) Draw an annotated sketch of the cliff identifying the key features (slope, vegetation, and so on) (c) Measure the shape of the cliff using a clinometer or protractor (d) Calculate the height of the cliff (by mathematical calculation or using an Ordnance Survey map)

Data collection

- Select an appropriate coastal site or two contrasting coastal sites.
- At each site collect the appropriate data.
- Take photographs or complete sketches to illustrate data collection methods and the physical characteristics at each site.

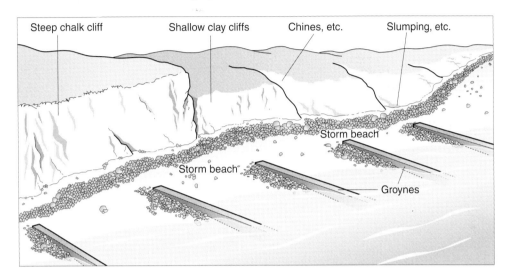

Presenting physical geography investigations

Possible data presentation methods for physical geography investigations include:

- a location map
- an annotated data collection map
- annotated sketches
- located and annotated photographs
- proportional symbol maps
- cross-section diagrams
- line graphs (flow data)
- bar graphs.

Be aware of the risks associated with collecting data in physical environments:

- Always discuss your data collection with teachers and parents.
- Inform people of when and where you are collecting information.
- Take a mobile phone with you and don't collect data alone.
- Look out for any warning signs.
- Wear appropriate clothing – conditions can change quickly!

4 Organising your coursework

Having collected the data required, you are now ready to begin putting it all together. Before you start, you will need to think about an overall structure and consider what you want your finished work to look like. The following points are worth considering:

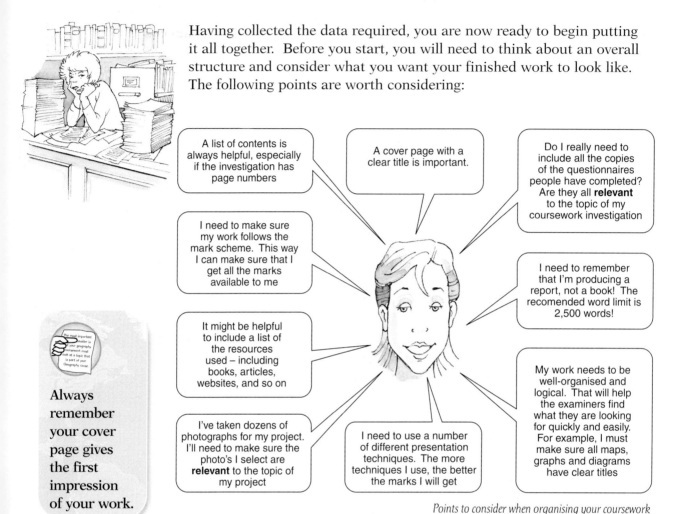

A list of contents is always helpful, especially if the investigation has page numbers

A cover page with a clear title is important.

Do I really need to include all the copies of the questionnaires people have completed? Are they all **relevant** to the topic of my coursework investigation

I need to make sure my work follows the mark scheme. This way I can make sure that I get all the marks available to me

I need to remember that I'm producing a report, not a book! The recomended word limit is 2,500 words!

It might be helpful to include a list of the resources used – including books, articles, websites, and so on

My work needs to be well-organised and logical. That will help the examiners find what they are looking for quickly and easily. For example, I must make sure all maps, graphs and diagrams have clear titles

I've taken dozens of photographs for my project. I'll need to make sure the photo's I select are **relevant** to the topic of my project

I need to use a number of different presentation techniques. The more techniques I use, the better the marks I will get

Points to consider when organising your coursework

Always remember your cover page gives the first impression of your work.

Organisational structure

There are different ways of organising your investigation – the following example might give you a few ideas!

Cover page

A map or photograph often helps to set the scene. For example, a study about a shopping centre could use a photograph of the area on a busy day.

Contents page

A contents page is a good way of showing that your investigation is well organised and logical. This will help the examiner find the information he or she is looking for quickly and easily.

It is better to do the contents page last – when you know how many pages you have used!

Introduction

The first section in most investigations is an introduction, which usually:

➲ describes what the investigation is about and gives some general background to the topic

➲ locates the investigation by using maps.

EXAMINER'S COMMENT

"In the better investigations it was very clear what the study was aiming to do and it was clearly linked to a part of the GCSE course. These investigations always used accurate maps to locate the study.

In the weaker investigations it was not always easy to identify the purpose of the study and it was only located with badly drawn maps without scales or north points."

Methodology

After the introduction it is helpful to include a methodology section. This should describe and explain the information you needed to carry out your investigation and say how you collected it.

EXAMINER'S COMMENT

"In the best investigations candidates not only described their data collection methods but also explained why they were important to the study. They also collected a good range of data."

Presentation and analysis

This section is where you present each part of your collected data and say what it means. You might have a large amount of data – try to use a variety of presentation methods. Describe *and* explain what your data shows.

EXAMINER'S COMMENT

"In the best investigations candidates use a variety of accurate techniques, including some more complex skills.

In the weaker investigations candidates often repeat a number of basic techniques such as bar charts."

Summary analysis

Having presented all of your data and identified the main points from it, it is useful to write a brief summary analysis. This helps to:

- ⮑ identify the important links between the different sets of data
- ⮑ identify the most important points you have found out
- ⮑ link the most important points to your original title.

EXAMINER'S COMMENT

"In the best investigations candidates described _and_ explained their data and identified detailed links between the data collected. They then linked the key points to the original title and used these to come to a sound conclusion."

Conclusion

A conclusion is an opportunity to:

- ⮑ return to the original idea or title
- ⮑ use the most useful parts of your data to:
  - – answer your original question
  - – say whether your hypothesis was correct or not
  - – sum up the main points and come to a decision.

In some investigations it might be better to include the conclusion in the summary analysis.

Evaluation

Every investigation should end with an evaluation. This gives you the opportunity to:

➲ think about how well the investigation worked in relation to your title
➲ consider the strengths and weaknesses of your data collection
➲ suggest how your investigation could be developed.

EXAMINER'S COMMENT

"The most effective investigations made observations about the limitations of the methods and how this may have affected the conclusions. They also made points about the accuracy of the data collection and linked this to the results.

In the weaker investigations candidates simply listed the problems they had or described what they could have done."

Bibliography

To complete the investigation a list of resources used – a bibliography – is often helpful and gives a good impression about the amount of background reading you have done.

5 Getting the marks

Using the mark scheme to help you succeed

This chapter looks at each area of the mark scheme and identifies some of the important points which will help you score the highest marks.

Your work will be marked using a common mark scheme which has five key areas, each of equal value. Those areas are:

Applied understanding

- ➲ Background understanding of the topic
- ➲ Where the investigation fits into the general understanding of the topic
- ➲ Location of the investigation

Methodology

- ➲ Links the data collection methods to the topic
- ➲ Describes and explains the data collection methods
- ➲ Planning and organisation of the investigation

Data presentation

- ➲ Use of a number of presentation techniques
- ➲ Use of some more complicated techniques
- ➲ Use of ICT in the presentation of the investigation

Data interpretation

- ➲ Describes what is shown by the data collection
- ➲ Explains what is shown by the data collection
- ➲ Identifies links between the collected data to draw conclusions

---

Evaluation

- ➲ Describes any limitations of the data collection
- ➲ Discusses the accuracy of the results
- ➲ Makes observations about the validity of the conclusion

Self-assessment will help you to improve your work. Using the full mark scheme go through your work and see how it matches up in each of the marking areas. Identify the strengths and weaknesses of your investigation and think about what you need to reach the highest level in each area. Often small improvements can make a big difference to your final mark!

Applied understanding

Applied understanding means that you show a general understanding about the topic you are investigating and can use that understanding to show where your particular investigation fits in. For example:

➲ If your investigation is about an area of coastline, you will need to show that you have a general understanding about coastal processes, and features and the way that coastal areas are managed.

➲ If your investigation is about managing town centres, you will need to show that you have a general understanding about the reasons why town centres need to be managed and methods being used in other towns.

You can show applied understanding throughout your investigation, but especially in the introduction, analysis and conclusion where you link your findings to the original ideas.

The mark scheme – applied understanding

	Level 1 (1–2 marks)	Level 2 (3–4 marks)	Level 3 (5–6 marks)
Applied understanding	Brief description of the location General understanding of the topic Some geographical language	Investigation effectively located General background understanding clearly applied to the topic Use of geographical language	Detailed locational understanding Thorough description and understanding of the ideas applied to the topic Uses a wide range of geographical language

EXAMINER'S COMMENTS ABOUT APPLIED UNDERSTANDING

"Applied understanding can be shown in all sections but is important in the introduction and analysis sections."

"In the best work the general ideas are mentioned throughout the investigation."

"Copying from textbooks does not show applied understanding – linking text book material to the investigation does."

"Using a definition box to identify all the key words is a good idea – but the words must be appropriate to the investigation."

"The use of annotated maps is an excellent way of both locating an investigation and identifying the key points."

The best way to make sure that you understand the topic being investigated is to do some background reading! Use textbooks to read up about the topic and look at any examples used – they may be similar to your investigation. At the same time make a note of any useful and appropriate words and definitions. Don't forget to make a note of any textbooks used so you can include them in your bibliography!

The following examples are introductions from three different investigations. Read them carefully and identify where they show applied understanding about their individual topics. The examiner's comments will help you to think about the strengths and weaknesses of each introduction.

Example 1

"This geography investigation is about Bowness-on-Windermere in the Lake District National Park. The aim of the study is to see if it is a honey pot site and to see if this causes any problems. A honey pot is a place where the scenery is very attractive or there are man-made features that interest people. This makes people swarm to the area – like bees to honey. There are many problems that can occur in a honey pot site including traffic jams, overcrowding, noise and litter and conflicts with local people.

It is important to study these areas because both local people and visitors can be affected. The environment can be spoiled, but at the same time visitors bring in money and create jobs."

(There was then a photocopy of a page from a textbook and a very basic map.)

EXAMINER'S COMMENT

"The investigation is located using description - the map was of little use. The candidate shows understanding and defines 'honey pot' effectively. The idea of conflict is expressed and also a number of pressures are described. It is a good attempt and has all the basic points.

It could be developed by expanding the general ideas, using maps to locate the area and saying exactly how the investigation is going to show whether Bowness-on-Windermere is a honey pot site."

Example 2

"The aim of this investigation is to find out if the quality of the environment and housing increases as you move from the centre of Surbiton to the edge. To do this, roads to the south of Surbiton were investigated."

(There was then a description of land-use models and a basic photocopied map with no annotations.)

EXAMINER'S COMMENT

"There is no real attempt to show the location of the investigation and although the idea is clear, there is limited detail. The reason for including the land-use models is not explained – they are just copied from a textbook and show no real understanding. Only looking at an area south of the town limits the use of the investigation. No geographical terminology is used."

If your investigation is 'issues-based', introduce the main issues in your introduction.

Example 3

"This investigation will consider whether Newport High Street should be pedestrianised, and relates to the 'Managing Town Centres' part of the GCSE Geography course. Pedestrianisation is the separation of people and traffic and is seen as a way of improving safety and general environmental quality in busy shopping areas. It is one way of managing movement in town centres and is increasingly common in the Central Business Districts (CBD) of busy towns.

Like many small historical towns, Newport has narrow streets and protected buildings and this makes pedestrianisation very difficult. The local council has been debating the issue for years, during which time growing traffic congestion has made the area increasingly dangerous and unattractive. As part of the main shopping and commercial area of Newport, the High Street attracts a lot of people and it is not unusual to see people having to walk in the road or between cars. Pedestrianisation seems like the obvious answer; however, local people and businesses are split over the issue because pedestrianisation will cause major disruption and traffic problems elsewhere because the High Street is a major route way. This investigation will use both primary and secondary evidence to consider the advantages and disadvantages of pedestrianisation and make a judgement about the issue."

(The candidate included a general location map and a detailed annotated map of the area. The candidate also identified the general advantages and disadvantages of pedestrianisation, gave some background to the area and identified key words.)

EXAMINER'S COMMENT

"This candidate has used the mark scheme really well. There are clear links to the GCSE course and an excellent level of understanding. It is very clear what the investigation is about and a good range of geographical terminology is used. The background information about the area is useful and the investigation is well located; the annotated map of the area was excellent."

Locating your investigation

Geography is always about place so it is important that you locate your investigation effectively. Always think: 'If someone who does not live in my area looked at my investigation, would they be able to work out exactly where it was?' Location can be described but using maps often makes it clearer and can get you presentation marks!

The following three examples show how an investigation can be located.

Which do you think is:

➲ the most effective?

➲ the most useful for your investigation?

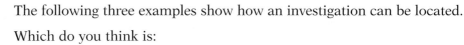

A nest of maps

In a site and situation map set, the situation map shows the general location and the site map highlights the study area.

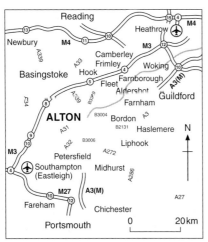

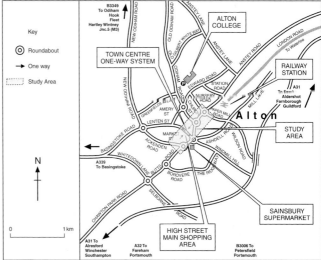

A site and situation map set

Annotated map showing area of investigation

The following investigation was about land-use change and the map gives excellent detail about the area and the topic – a good opportunity for ICT skills. However, it also needs a general location map to show where it is!

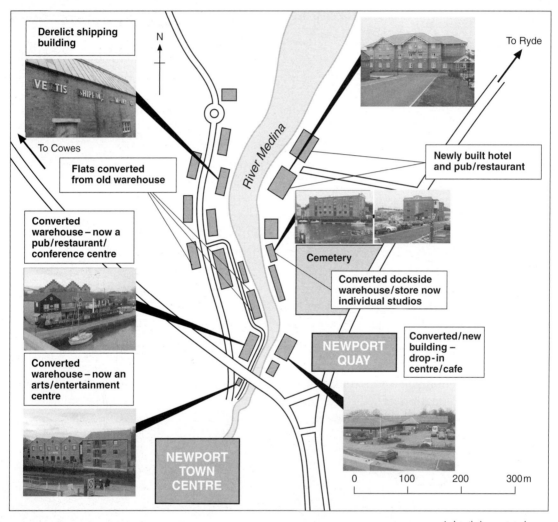

Derelict shipping building

N

To Ryde

To Cowes

River Medina

Newly built hotel and pub/restaurant

Flats converted from old warehouse

Converted warehouse – now a pub/restaurant/ conference centre

Cemetery

Converted dockside warehouse/store now individual studios

NEWPORT QUAY

Converted/new building – drop-in centre/cafe

Converted warehouse – now an arts/entertainment centre

NEWPORT TOWN CENTRE

0   100   200   300 m

A detailed annotated map

Remember to use titles, scales and north points on maps.

To find out more about **maps**, including Ordnance Survey maps, base/location maps, street maps, town centre use maps and old maps, go to www.heinemann.co.uk/hotlinks, insert the express code 0158P, and click on this topic.

Methodology

Methodology is about the methods used to carry out the investigation. This means that you need to say why you used the particular data collection methods in your investigation and explain how you collected the data.

The mark scheme – methodology

Methodology	Level 1 (1–2 marks)	Level 2 (3–4 marks)	Level 3 (5–6 marks)
	Basic links between the topic and data collection Lists methods of data collection Limited range of basic techniques	Data collection clearly linked to the topic Describes data collection methods Good range of appropriate techniques	Data collection has detailed links to the topic Describes and explains the relevance of data collection methods Wide range of appropriate techniques Evidence of originality and initiative

To get Level 3 marks in the methodology area, you will need to show 'originality and initiative', which means that you need some individual data which is unique to you. Individual data is not 'more of the same' – in other words, not another 20 questionnaires which are the same as the previous 100 carried out by a group of students! You need to collect some different data – it could be more primary data, but secondary data is also useful!

EXAMINER'S COMMENT

"In the most successful investigations candidates linked the data collection methods to the title of the investigation and explained carefully why each piece of data was required. They then went on to describe how the data was collected, including factors such as the reasons for the number of questionnaires or the location of pedestrian and traffic counts. The investigation was well organised with clearly headed sections.

In the weaker investigations candidates simply listed the methods of data collection and failed to explain why they were important to the investigation or how they were carried out."

If you try to get information by writing letters but receive no reply, you should mention this in your evaluation.

Important questions about your methodology

About techniques

Did you?

- ⮑ use a number (five or six) of different data collection methods
- ⮑ say why your data is important to your investigation
- ⮑ use primary and secondary data

About organisation

Did you:

- ⮑ include a title page
- ⮑ include a contents page
- ⮑ organise your work into clear sections
- ⮑ make sure every presentation has a heading

About originality/initiative

Did you:

- ⮑ identify and collect some of your own data

If not, is there any additional data that you could include to make your work 'individual'?

The following example is part of the methodology of an investigation about the Central Business District (CBD) of a large town.

"Pedestrian counts were carried out in ten locations selected at equal distances from the town centre to see if there is any relationship between the number of pedestrians and the distance from the town centre. Counts were taken for a period of five minutes and they were all carried out during the mid-afternoon period so that they were comparable.

A land-use survey was carried out by putting the shops and services into categories, walking around the town and marking them on a base map. At the same time it was noted whether the shops/services were national stores or local businesses. This was done to see if there was a relationship between the type of function and distance from the town centre."

EXAMINER'S COMMENT

"The candidate clearly shows why the data is important to the investigation and explains carefully how it was collected – including some points about sampling with the pedestrian counts".

Identify
clearly any
individual
data in your
methodology.

Useful methodology techniques

Methodology matrix

A methodology matrix, or table, is a way of listing the data collection methods and explaining how they were carried out. An example is shown below.

A methodology matrix

Method	Why required	How was it carried out?	Limitations
Pedestrian count	To identify how busy different parts of the town centre were	Ten sites were chosen at 100-metre intervals from the town centre. People were counted for five minutes during mid-afternoon	Data at other times of the day and other days of the week would be useful
Questionnaire	To get information about shopping habits and views about shopping quality	Fifty people were chosen at random	The sample could have been bigger. At the weekend there might have been a broader range of people

EXAMINER'S COMMENT

"Methodology tables can cover the what, why and how of the methods used, but you must make sure you include enough detail to get the highest marks!"

Methodology map

Where most of the primary data is collected in a small area, a methodology map is a useful technique to show the location of the data collection points.

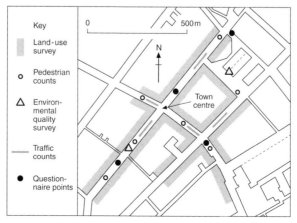

A methodology map

The presentation method must be appropriate for the data being displayed

What types of data presentation methods can be used?

Some methods, such as location maps, are appropriate for all investigations. The suitability of other methods will depend upon the type of investigation. The spider diagram below identifies some of the different types of presentation methods commonly used.

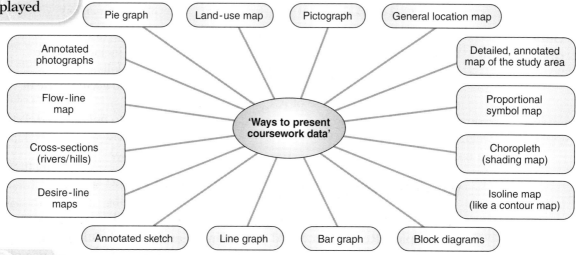

Data presentation methods

Look through textbooks to get ideas about presentation methods.

EXAMINER'S COMMENT

– "Attractive or colourful does not necessarily mean more complex!

– More complex skills include choropleth maps, proportional flow lines, located proportional symbol maps, detailed scattergraphs.

– Less complex skills include bar graphs, line graphs and pie graphs.

– Neatness and accuracy is important."

Maps must have titles, keys, scales and a north point.

Use of photographs can be:

➲ **basic** – includes simple annotations
➲ **more complex** – describes some features
➲ **complex** – located and includes detailed annotations.

Data interpretation

Data interpretation is where the collected data is explained and linked back to the original idea.

The key parts of data interpretation are:

- ⊃ describing the data – what does the data show?
- ⊃ explaining or suggesting reasons – why does it show this?
- ⊃ drawing out links between the data and the topic of your coursework in a conclusion.

What does this mean?

The following examples are from a town centre study. It included pedestrian counts and a land-use survey as part of the data collection.

Examples

Describe: "Outside of Woolworths 220 pedestrians were counted in five minutes."

Explain: "Outside of Woolworths 220 pedestrians were counted in five minutes. This is a high number because Woolworths is a major department store near the town centre."

Links: "Outside of Woolworths 220 pedestrians were counted in five minutes. This is a high number because Woolworth's is a major department store and the land-use survey clearly shows that it is in the Central Business District which usually attracts the most people."

You can show applied understanding in this section by linking your investigation to general ideas about the topic.

The mark scheme – data interpretation

	Level 1 (1–2 marks)	Level 2 (3–4 marks)	Level 3 (5–6 marks)
Data interpretation	Brief description of results	Good description of results Gives meaning to the results Some concluding points	Detailed description of results with clear reasons Draws out links between data Concluding points linked to original title

If you have explained each part of your data collection separately, it is a good idea to write a 'summary' interpretation to identify any links between the data.

The importance of a proper conclusion

The conclusion is an opportunity to:

- ⊃ return to the original title/idea/theory
- ⊃ bring the investigation together by reflecting back to the original aim of the investigation
- ⊃ identify the most important parts of the data collection
- ⊃ identify the important links between the different sets of data
- ⊃ show applied understanding by illustrating how the investigation is similar to textbook examples.

It is useful to start the conclusion by re-stating the aims of the investigation. For example: 'The aim of this investigation was ...'

If the investigation is:

- ⊃ a **question** – make sure that you have answered it
- ⊃ a **hypothesis** – make it clear whether it has been proved or not
- ⊃ an **issue** – make sure that you have identified both sides of the argument
- ⊃ linked to a **theory** – make sure that you draw a clear comparison with the original theory.

EXAMINER'S COMMENT

"The most successful investigations identified the main points from the data and suggested clear reasons for the results of the data collection. They then went on to identify the important links between the data and used these to return to the original idea and reach a conclusion. Observations were then made about how the investigation compared with similar examples elsewhere or in text books.

In weaker investigations the data was not presented very neatly or accurately and although each set of data was described, there were no real reasons suggested for the patterns shown by the data, and conclusions were limited."

The following example shows part of the data interpretation of an investigation about the influence of tourism on the Central Business District in Canterbury (Kent). (Each method of data collection had a separate interpretation.)

Use the examiner's comments below to identify any strengths.

Example

"Interpretation of land-use data

The land-use map shows that there is a concentration of gift shops and tourist-related shops near to the cathedral, with over 20 tourist-related shops within 100 metres. This contrasts with national stores which tend to be less concentrated closer to the cathedral. Also close to the cathedral is a concentration of cafes and restaurants. It is clear that both the gift shops and cafes are trying to capitalise on the large number of tourists visiting the area while national stores are less significant here since most tourists don't visit the area to use shops that probably exist in their home towns.

Conclusion

It is clear that Canterbury does not have a typical Central Business District (CBD) as seen in many towns and described in textbook models. The town is partly dominated by the tourist trade and the land use reflects this. Thousands of people visit the cathedral from all over the world (see the sphere of influence map) and visitors demand souvenirs and refreshments. Consequently, there is a higher than typical number of tourist-related activities and many more cafes than might be expected of a place the size of Canterbury. Other places that have major historical visitor attractions might have a similar type of land-use structure; comparing Canterbury with Winchester or York might be an interesting exercise. However, although visitors generate a lot of money and jobs in Canterbury, the questionnaire suggested that some local people feel that the range of shopping facilities for local residents is not very satisfactory."

EXAMINER'S COMMENT

"This candidate has described and explained the collected data in detail and has identified clear links between the data. There is reference to the presented data (land-use map, sphere of influence map, questionnaire) and some use of geographical terminology. The conclusion returns to the aim of the investigation and uses evidence from the data to make key points. The conclusion also shows applied understanding by comparing Canterbury with 'typical' areas and bringing in comparisons with other places."

Always use the most appropriate statistical methods in relation to the investigation.

Data interpretation – using statistics

Data is often collected in the form of statistics, some of which is quite straightforward and some very complicated.

There are a number of simple ways of describing statistics including:

- calculating averages
- calculating the median (the middle value of ranked data)
- calculating the mode (the most frequently occurring number)
- describing the minimum and maximum numbers
- calculating the statistical range (largest minus smallest).
- drawing a dispersion diagram

Using statistics to explain relationships between data

Example of a dispersion diagram

Statistical techniques can be used to describe and explain the relationship between two sets of data. Look at the following example, which is part of an investigation about shopping patterns in a town centre, and think about whether these techniques might be useful in your investigation.

Question – How often do you visit the following shopping areas each month? Each dot represents one person.

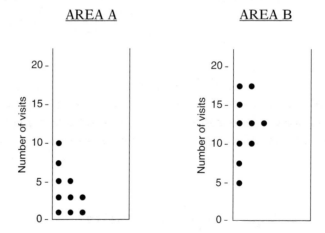

Using statistics: an example of a shopping investigation

Aim: To see if the number of pedestrians decreases with the distance from a town centre.

Data collection method: Ten locations were chosen at varying distances from the town centre. At each location the number of pedestrians was counted over a five-minute period.

Collected data for shopping investigation

Location	1	2	3	4	5	6	7	8	9	10
Distance from town centre (m)	10	50	100	80	70	200	150	400	300	250
Number of pedestrains (nearest 10)	320	280	270	260	290	200	210	90	190	170

Presenting the data in a scattergraph

To draw a scattergraph:

1 Draw and label the two axis.
2 Choose scales to cover the range of data.
3 Plot the data using dots.
4 Put on a line of best fit (do not just join up the dots!).

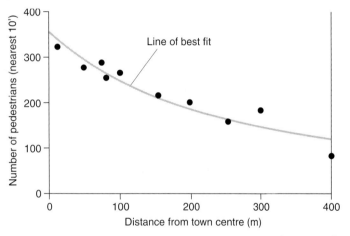

A scattergraph

What does a scattergraph show?

➲ **Positive relationship** – as one data set increases, so does the other.
➲ **Negative relationship** – as one data set increases, the other decreases.
➲ **No relationship** – no real pattern is evident, so the relationship is unproven.

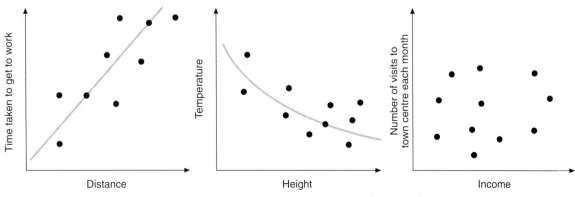

Scattergraph showing a positive relationship   *Scattergraph showing a negative relationship*   *Scattergraph showing a no relationship*

What does the scattergraph of the shopping investigation data suggest?

1 There is a negative relationship – the number of pedestrians falls as distance from the town centre increases.

2 It is quite a strong relationship since all the dots are close to the line of best fit.

3 Some dots do not quite fit the pattern (explain why).

Testing the strength of a relationship

Looking at the scattergraph of the shopping investigation data, it is clear that the two sets of data are related. The strength of a relationship between two sets of data is called a **correlation**. This can be calculated using the Spearman Rank Correlation Coefficient (RS). This is a statistical calculation which always gives a result from -1 (negative correlation) to $+1$ (positive correlation); the nearer to 1 the stronger the link between the data.

How do you calculate RS?

1 Rank both sets of data from the highest to the lowest.

Distance from town centre	Rank	Number of pedestrains	Rank	Difference between ranks (d)	d^2
400	1	90	10	9	81
300	2	190	8	6	36
250	3	170	9	6	36
200	4	200	7	3	9
150	5	210	6	1	1
100	6	270	4	2	4
80	7	260	5	2	4
70	8	290	2	6	36
50	9	280	3	6	36
10	10	320	1	9	81
					Total (Σ) = 324

2 Use the formula:

$$RS = \frac{1-6}{n^3} - n$$

where:
d = difference between ranks
n = number of observations
Σ = total d^2

3 Using the example above:

$$RS = 1 - \frac{6 \times 324}{10^3} - 10$$

$$= 1 - \frac{1944}{990}$$

$$= 1 - 1.96$$

$$= -0.96$$

4 This shows that there is a very strong negative relationship between the number of pedestrians and the distance from the town centre. In other words as you move away from the town centre the number of pedestrians decreases.

Only use scattergraphs or correlation where it is appropriate.

Evaluation

Evaluation is about reflecting upon how effectively the investigation addressed the original idea and making observations about how it could be improved or developed.

The mark scheme – evaluation

	Level 1 (1–2 marks)	Level 2 (3–4 marks)	Level 3 (5–6 marks)
Evaluation	Some appreciation of how the investigation could be improved Comments on the reliability of the methods	Clear appreciation of how the investigation could be improved Comments on the reliability of the methods Comments on the accuracy of the results	Comments on the reliability of the methods Comments on the accuracy of the results Comments on the validity of the conclusion

The three elements of the evaluation pathway are shown below. It is always worth starting by looking at the methods, because it is usually limitations in the methods that affect the results and conclusions.

Evaluation is not just about listing what else could have been done.

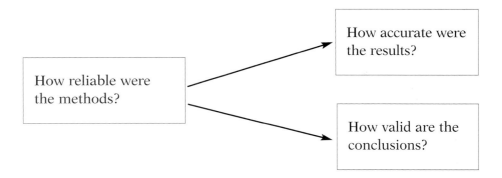

How reliable were the methods? → How accurate were the results?

How reliable were the methods? → How valid are the conclusions?

Since you are evaluating your work in terms of how well it has satisfied the original aim, begin by quoting the aim.

A useful start is to ask yourself the following questions:

- How effective was the data in addressing the original aim of the investigation?
- Should I have collected data at different times of the day or week?
- Did the weather affect my results?
- Did I use enough questionnaires?
- How accurate were the data collection methods?
- What other data might have been useful?
- What was the most/least useful data?
- Were there any particular problems in collecting the data?
- How could the methods have been improved?
- Did the lack of data or data collection problems affect the conclusions?

It might be helpful to organise your evaluation into three sections:
1   Evaluation of methods.
2   Accuracy of results.
3   Validity of conclusions.

EXAMINER'S COMMENT

"The key to a successful evaluation is to link the three evaluative elements together in the following way:
1 Identify the limitations of the <u>methods</u>.
2 Say how this led to <u>inaccurate results</u>.
3 Explain how using inaccurate results might lead to <u>invalid conclusions</u>."

The following examples show part of the evaluation from two town centre investigations. The examiner's comments will help you identify their strengths and weaknesses.

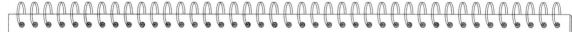

Example

"My Richmond project was of great use for my own knowledge. Despite the bad weather it was a great success and I collected lots of information, although I did not fully realise why I was doing it. I think the results were reliable. It could be improved by spending more time on it."

EXAMINER'S COMMENT

"This is just a vague statement which says nothing about particular data and makes very general points. It does not evaluate anything."

Example

"The quality of information from secondary sources was disappointing. Local estate agents had no information about the past growth of the town, which meant that I had to use observation to date housing. This could have been inaccurate and, consequently, conclusions about the growth of the town incorrect. This was not helped by the fact that the library only had the 2001 Census data, although more time at the planning office might have been useful.

Conducting my questionnaire on a Saturday could have given a false impression because it is not a working day and is also market day. Consequently, any conclusions about the sphere of influence may not give a completely accurate picture."

EXAMINER'S COMMENT

"There is a clear reference to limitations of the methods and how these affected both levels of accuracy and validity of conclusion. Also problems of data collection are evident and observations about how data collection methods might be improved."

Evaluation techniques

An evaluation grid can be used to make comments about each set of collected data. An example is shown below.

Evaluation grid

Method	Reliability of method	Accuracy of results	Validity of conclusions
Pedestrian count	Quite reliable, although may have missed people	Only completed on a weekday. Only completed once during the day	Limited data to draw conclusions. Need for data on different days/times of the day

This is a useful technique but can lack detail. Consequently, it might be helpful to write a summary evaluation identifying the main points in more detail.

6 Coursework ideas

Investigating residential areas in towns

Investigations about residential areas in towns could include:

- ➲ an assessment of different residential areas in a town
- ➲ an assessment about how residential areas change with distance from a town centre
- ➲ comparing residential land-use patterns with textbook theories
- ➲ considering a local planning/redevelopment issue
- ➲ testing a hypothesis such as 'The quality of residential areas increases with distance from a town centre'.

There are a number of different types of residential areas in towns. These areas vary in terms of age, type, quality and price of housing. Some areas are more popular than others because of their facilities or because they have a more positive reputation. In order to investigate residential areas the following points will need to be considered:

- ➲ housing quality
- ➲ general environmental quality
- ➲ building densities
- ➲ local amenities
- ➲ traffic flow and congestion (safety issues)
- ➲ perception of different areas – what people think.

Care needs to be taken when dealing with personal and sensitive questions!

Possible sources of data

Primary	Secondary
Land-use survey	Textbooks
Housing quality index	Maps (local/Ordnance Survey)
General environmental quality survey	Census data (very useful)
Traffic counts	Local planning data
Questionnaires of local residents	Local newspaper articles
Interviews with local residents	Estate agents
Interview with local planner	Websites
Housing density index	
Children's play space survey	
Amenity index	
Photographs	

Make a note of all secondary sources used so that they can be included in the bibliography.

Investigating town centres

Investigations about town centres or the influence of town centres could include:

- ➲ investigating urban land use and change
- ➲ identifying or delimiting specific areas such as the Central Business District (CBD)
- ➲ calculating the sphere of influence of a town
- ➲ investigating particular urban issues such as traffic congestion, parking problems, pedestrianisation or land-use change
- ➲ assessing a local planning issue such as a redevelopment scheme
- ➲ comparing an urban area with textbook theories
- ➲ testing a hypothesis such as 'The CBD attracts more people because it has a greater number of functions' or 'The larger a town, the greater its sphere of influence'.

There are many opportunities for investigations about town centres or the influence of town centres and a wide range of possible data collection opportunities. The following list gives a number of possible sources of data – obviously the data required will be determined by the specific topic being investigated.

Make sure you have a clear title and the data collection methods are linked to the title.

Possible sources of data

Primary	Secondary
Land-use survey	Textbooks
Survey of local/national business	Local maps
Pedestrian count	Ordnance Survey maps
Traffic count	Local planning data
Building height survey	Local newspaper articles
Land-use transect	Estate agents
Parking survey	Websites
Questionnaires	Census data
Interviews	
Environmental quality survey	
Building age survey	
Photographs	
Sketches	

When deciding on the methods of data collection always consider how the data could be presented. Will your data give you the opportunity to use a range of presentation methods?

To find out more about **traffic management** and **traffic flow data**, go to www.heinemann.co.uk/hotlinks, insert the express code 0158P, and click on this topic.

To find out more about **air quality data**, go to www.heinemann.co.uk/hotlinks, insert the express code 0158P, and click on this topic.

Investigating changing industrial areas

Investigations about changing industrial areas could include:

⮞ assessing industrial change in a local area
⮞ investigating why industry develops in particular areas
⮞ a question such as 'Why has industry moved to the edge of towns?' or 'What is the impact of the growth of an industrial estate?'
⮞ comparing industrial location with textbook theories
⮞ testing a hypothesis such as 'Industrial estates are as much about retailing as industry'
⮞ comparing the advantages and disadvantages of town centre and edge of town sites.

Industrial estates have developed on the edge of many towns in the past 30 years. These are usually purpose built with car parking and road links and are usually separated from residential areas. Increasingly, other functions have developed on some of these sites, including car showrooms, large warehouse stores and leisure developments. Some of the reasons for this are:

⮞ a lack of development space in town centres
⮞ the high cost of land in town centres
⮞ problems of traffic congestion in town centres
⮞ planning restrictions
⮞ the increasing need for parking space for staff and customers.

Possible sources of data

Primary	Secondary
Land-use survey	Textbooks
Interviews with business managers	Maps (local/Ordnance Survey)
Questionnaires – staff, customers, local residents	Local planning data
Traffic surveys	Local newspapers
Parking surveys	Local business directories
Environmental quality survey – congestion, litter, landscaping	Websites

Think of a title that clearly expresses the idea of the investigation.

Investigating tourism

Investigations about tourism could include:

⮑ assessing the affect of tourism in an area
⮑ an assessment of one particular effect (environmental or economic)
⮑ examining a local issue or proposed development
⮑ assessing how effectively a honey pot area is managed
⮑ testing a hypothesis such as whether a place could be classified as a honey pot
⮑ a question such as 'Is tourism more trouble than it is worth?'

Tourism can have a number of impacts on an area – some of which might be positive and others negative. In order to investigate the impact of tourism a number of factors could be considered, some of which are shown below.

Economic factors	Social factors	Environmental factors
Jobs created by tourism	The effect on local services	Increased traffic
Money brought into the area	Conflicts between tourists and local people	Overcrowding
Increased trade for local shops and services	Seasonal employment	Litter
The effect on house prices	The effect on behaviour and crime	Land-use change
		Erosion of footpaths

Possible sources of data

Primary	Secondary
Land-use survey to identify tourism-related facilities	Textbooks
	Maps (local/Ordnance Survey)
Interviews with local business	Local directories (tourist facilities)
Questionnaires – local people, tourists	Local council
Photographs	Local planning data
Environmental quality survey – litter, noise, footpath erosion	Tourist information centre
	Local newspaper articles
Traffic counts	Estate agents (house price survey/number of holiday homes)
Parking survey – at different times	
Pedestrian count – at different times	Websites

Use photographs to describe key points – include annotations to explain them!

To find out more about **coastal resorts**, go to www.heinemann.co.uk/hotlinks, insert the express code 0158P, and click on this topic.

To find out more about **beach quality**, go to www.heinemann.co.uk/hotlinks, insert the express code 0158P, and click on this topic.

To find out more about **National Parks**, go to www.heinemann.co.uk/hotlinks, insert the express code 0158P, and click on this topic.

To find out more about **Nature reserves**, go to www.heinemann.co.uk/hotlinks, insert the express code 0158P, and click on this topic.

To find out more about **environmental data**, go to www.heinemann.co.uk/hotlinks, insert the express code 0158P, and click on this topic.

Glossary

Analysis – explaining data and identifying relationships

Annotate – add notes to maps, diagrams, sketches, photographs

Bibliography – a list of secondary data sources

Central business district – the commercial centre of a settlement

Chloropleth map – a map that uses shading density to show different values

Clinometer – an instrument used to measure the angle of a slope

Correlation – the relationship between two sets of data

Cost-benefit analysis – a list of the costs and benefits of a planning project, used to make a decision

Data – information collected by primary or secondary research

Desire line – a line that represents the movement of people from one place to another

Evaluation – assessing how efficiently an investigation has been carried out

Hypothesis – a statement about a particular topic that can be proved or disproved

High-order goods – expensive goods which are not bought frequently

Interpretation – identifying what data is showing

Isoline map – a map using lines which join up data of equal value

Land-use map – a map showing the different types of land-use in an area

Methodology – the methods used to collect data in order to carry out an investigation

Objective data – data not subject to opinions

Primary data – data gathered by direct observation, measurement or questioning

Proportional symbol map – a map which uses proportional, located symbols to show data

Sampling – selecting a particular group of people or data to represent a whole situation

Scattergraph – plotting two sets of data to establish a relationship

Secondary data – published data from books, newspapers, websites, and so on

Sphere of influence – the area served by a settlement or which it has economic influence over

Subjective data – data which is based upon people's views and opinions

Tabulate – arrange data in a table

Talking heads – a technique of using heads and speech bubbles to show people's opinions

Transect – a line used to gather data, either on a map or on the ground